RUGBY F⊕CUS

PLAYERS AND SKILLS

Jon Richards

WAYLAND

First published in 2015 by Wayland

Dewey Number: 796.3'33-dc22
ISBN: 978 0 7502 9481 2
Library ebook ISBN: 978 0 7502 7665 8

10 9 8 7 6 5 4 3 2 1

MIX
Paper from responsible sources
FSC
www.fsc.org
FSC® C104740

Editor: Camilla Lloyd
Produced by Tall Tree Ltd
Editor, Tall Tree: Jennifer Sanderson
Designer: Ben Ruocco
Consultant: Tony Buchanan

Wayland
An imprint of
Hachette Children's Group
Part of Hodder & Stoughton
Carmelite House
50 Victoria Embankment
London EC4Y 0DZ

Printed in China

An Hachette UK Company

www.hachette.co.uk

www.hachettechildrens.co.uk

Acknowledgements
The author and publisher would like to thank the
following people for their help and participation
in this book: Old Albanian RFC and Neil Dekker.

Picture credits
All photograpphy by Michael Wicks, except for:
2, 11, 24 bottom left, 30 Graphitec/Dreamstime.com,
4, 5, 6, 9, 14, 18, 19 bottom, 20, 23 bottom right
Santamarad/Dreamstime.com, 7 Rixie/Dreamstime.com,
13t Melis82/Dreamstime.com, 15 bottom Maccers/
Dreamstime.com, 16, 22 bottom right Dgoodings/
Dreamstime.com, 28 Agno_agnus/Dreamstime.com

CONTENTS

A sport of skill

Rugby is a high-energy sport that involves physical contact. Players try to tackle each other, win possession of the ball and use their skills to score the most points.

Individual and group skills

A rugby team consists of 15 players and each player uses specific skills during a match. These skills depend on the situations in which players find themselves. At certain times, players need to work together in units to perform attacking or defending moves as well as set-pieces. Set-pieces are the moves used to restart play and include scrums and lineouts.

While all players need to be able to pass and catch the ball, a scrum-half also needs to be able to spin pass the ball quickly and accurately.

Female players from Spanish team Getxo (left) and French team Perpignan (right) compete during a lineout. A lineout involves a collection of individual skills, such as throwing in, jumping and lifting. However, the players have to combine these skills and work as a unit to win possession of the ball and to launch an attack.

Core skills

Many children start playing rugby at a very young age, sometimes as young as six years old. At this level, full contact is not allowed. Instead, they play tag rugby, where players pull on tags tucked into opponents' shorts to 'tackle' them. Young players will first learn passing and catching skills as well as the ability to run into spaces in the opposition defence. These skills are important to all forms of rugby and used by players at all levels, right up to international matches. As players get older, they start to add new skills, including tackling, lifting in the lineout and scrummaging.

> " *The whole point of rugby is that it is, first and foremost, a state of mind, a spirit.* "
>
> Former French player
> **Jean-Pierre Rives**

Rugby fit

Rugby players need to be very fit so that they perform to the best of their ability for an entire match. Players work hard to improve their fitness and to increase their body strength.

Work hard, play hard

Rugby players spend many hours each week training to improve their performance. This includes practising outdoors to develop moves and skills. Under the guidance of a coach, players will take part in specific drills designed to improve individual parts of a game, such as the lineout or an attacking move. Players also work hard in the gym, lifting weights, to improve their strength. Being physically strong helps to prepare the body for the effects of playing a contact sport.

BALL IN HAND

New Zealand's Sean Fitzpatrick holds the record for playing the most international matches in a row without injury: he played in a run of 63 consecutive rugby games.

Warming up before a match raises the heart rate and prepares the body for exercise. Here, players from French team, RC Narbonne, are doing short runs to warm up before a match.

Serious injuries can see players out of action for months and result in them missing out on crucial matches. This physiotherapist is treating a player of London Wasps to see if he is fit enough to continue playing.

Preventing injuries

At older age levels, rugby is a full-contact sport and bumps, bruises and other injuries are a part of playing it. Keeping fit and improving their strength can help players prevent serious injuries. Injuries could see them forced to leave a match and could put players out of action for a long time. Damage to joints, such as the knees and shoulders, are among the most common injuries in rugby. Strengthening the legs and arms can help to reduce the risk of injury to these body parts.

Playing positions: forwards

A rugby team is divided up into two groups of players: forwards and backs. The forwards are numbered one to eight and during a match, they take part in scrums and lineouts.

Forward positions

The forwards are divided up into three groups, depending on where they form up for a scrum (see pages 28–29). Players wearing numbers one to three are called the front row. Numbers four and five stand behind the front row in the scrum – they are known as the second row. Behind the second row are the flankers (they stand on the flanks, or sides, of the scrum) and the number eight, who stands at the rear of the scrum.

BALL IN HAND

New Zealand prop Richie McCaw holds the record for the most international appearances by a forward. Since 2001 he has played 137 times for New Zealand.

While some players can play in both the second and back row, the front row must be made up of props and a hooker. Scrummaging can be dangerous and only specialists in these positions can play here.

1. Prop (front row)
2. Hooker (front row)
3. Prop (front row)
4. Second row
5. Second row
6. Flanker (back row)
7. Flanker (back row)
8. Number eight (back row)

The forwards from London Irish (in white) and Perpignan (in black) have set a scrum. Each hooker stands between his team's props and the three of them bind together. The second rows bind together and join the front row. Binding together as a unit is one of the most important factors in scrummaging.

Forward play

The forwards play in set-pieces, such as scrums and lineouts. They are also involved in the short passages of play that occur after a player has been tackled. These passages are known as break-downs and include rucks and mauls (see page 20–21). Forward play requires a lot of strength and, as such, forwards tend to be larger than backs. Back-row players need to be the first players to get to a break-down. They work hard on improving their fitness so that they can cover as much of the pitch as possible during a match. Front row and second row players need to be strong so that they can push in scrums, rucks and mauls.

Playing positions: backs

The backs wear numbers nine to 15. They usually form a line standing away from the scrum, lineout or break-down, ready to attack or to defend against any opposition attacks.

The back line

The scrum-half is usually the first back to arrive at a break-down. He acts as the link between the forwards and the backs. The fly-half usually decides the type of attack to be carried out. Outside the fly-half stand the centres. They carry out attacking runs and usually form the first line of defence against opposition attacks. The wingers are usually fast runners and are used to finish off attacking moves. The full-back can be brought into attacking moves and also acts as the last line of defence.

BALL IN HAND

Irish centre Brian O'Driscoll holds the record for the most international appearances. Between 1999 and 2014 he appeared 141 times for Ireland and the British and Irish Lions.

During a match, the backs move around and form up in response to where the ball is and where the opposition defenders are standing.

9.	Scrum-half
10.	Fly-half
11.	Left wing
12.	Centre
13.	Centre
14.	Right wing
15.	Full-back

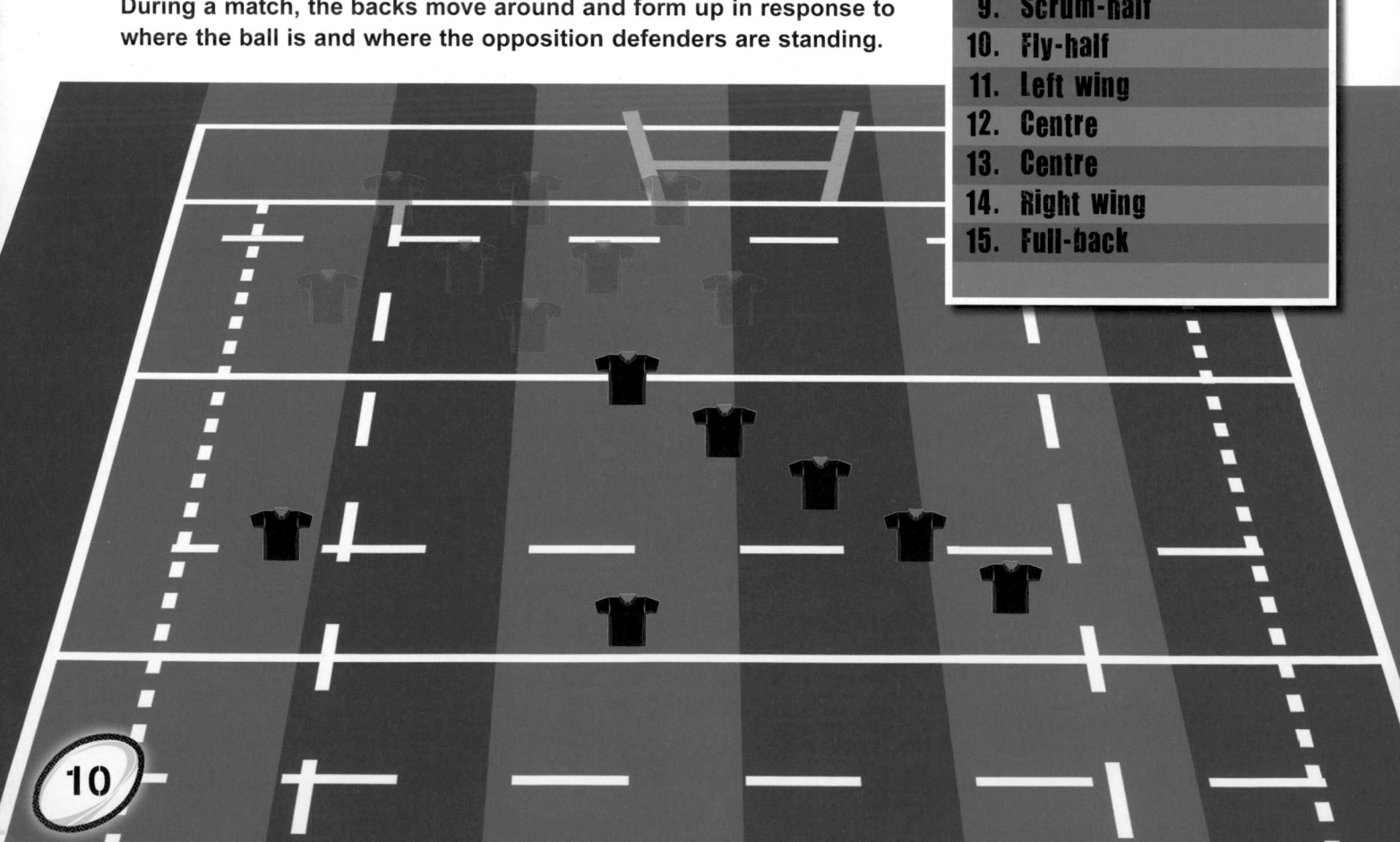

Back play

Backs need to be fast so that they can perform attacking moves quickly and chase down any opposition attackers. They should also have good passing and catching skills and be able to kick the ball accurately from their hands. Backs may find themselves without the ball for periods of time while the forwards battle for possession and position. However, they should still remain alert as the ball could come their way at a moment's notice or the opposition could steal possession and launch a surprise attack.

Munster and Ireland player, Keith Earls, is capable of playing several back positions. Such players are called 'utility backs'.

Player power
Backs should work hard to develop their speed during training sessions. Running speed can be improved with short-distance sprints.

Passing and receiving

Good passing moves the ball around the pitch quickly and away from the opposition. Passes should always be backwards. A forward pass will see a scrum awarded to the opposition.

Passing and catching skills

Players usually pass the ball while they are running. They have to think about their speed and where their team-mates are on the pitch, so that they can pass the ball accurately. They also need to judge how hard to throw a pass.

Lateral pass

1 The player receiving a pass must keep his eyes on the ball at all times. He needs to hold out his hands to give the player passing the ball a target at which to aim.

2 The receiver then turns his head to face the next player in the line, who keeps his arms out ready for the pass.

3 The passer throws the ball smoothly backwards to his team-mate, judging the speed and force of his throw to make sure he does not overthrow it.

A player from Romanian team Dinamo Bucaresti has managed to pass the ball away to a team-mate just before he is tackled. He has kept his eyes on his team-mate rather than looking at the player who is about to tackle him.

Passing variations

There are several different types of pass, each of which is used in a different situation. For example, a short pop pass is used to pass to a team-mate who is running close by in support. A spin pass is used to throw the ball accurately and quickly over a long distance. The player spins the ball by putting his hands on either side of it and then flicking his wrists so that the ball spins along its length.

The scrum-half spin passes the ball away from a break-down. The spin pass is an effective way to move the ball away from defending forwards to your own team's back line.

Running with the ball

The correct running technique allows players to be aware of those around them. This means that they can spot gaps, and change direction quickly while keeping hold of the ball.

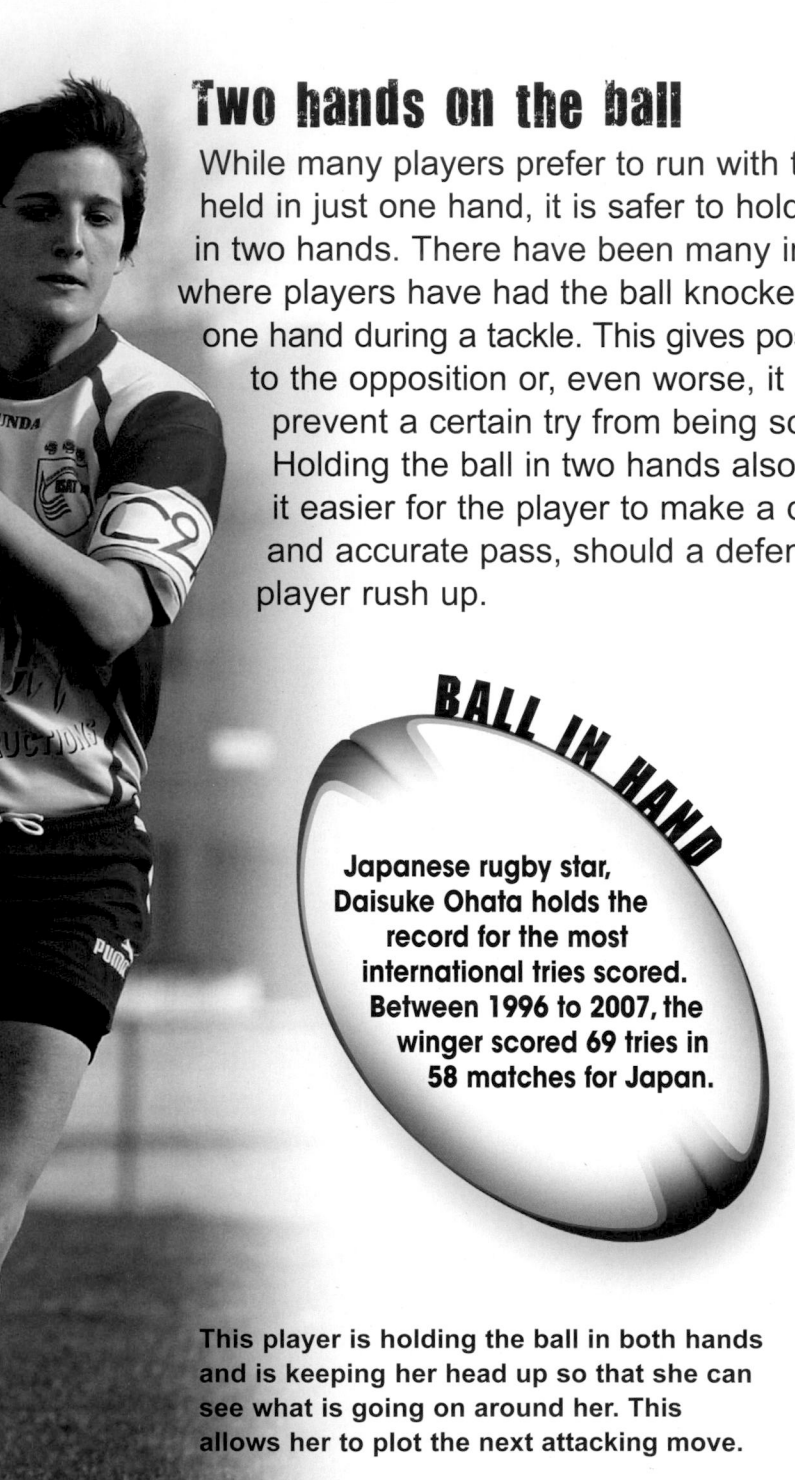

Two hands on the ball

While many players prefer to run with the ball held in just one hand, it is safer to hold the ball in two hands. There have been many instances where players have had the ball knocked out of one hand during a tackle. This gives possession to the opposition or, even worse, it can prevent a certain try from being scored. Holding the ball in two hands also makes it easier for the player to make a quick and accurate pass, should a defensive player rush up.

BALL IN HAND

Japanese rugby star, Daisuke Ohata holds the record for the most international tries scored. Between 1996 to 2007, the winger scored 69 tries in 58 matches for Japan.

This player is holding the ball in both hands and is keeping her head up so that she can see what is going on around her. This allows her to plot the next attacking move.

Dodging and weaving

Many rugby players can use changes of pace or direction to trick opponents and to create openings. A player may use a side-step where he plants one foot firmly on the floor while he is running, and uses it to push away in a different direction. A swerve is not as extreme as a side-step, but it can also be an effective way to change direction. In a swerve, a player, having leaned in one direction, takes a step across his body and leans away to veer around an opponent. Other tactics involve faking certain moves, such as throwing a dummy pass.

Dummy passes

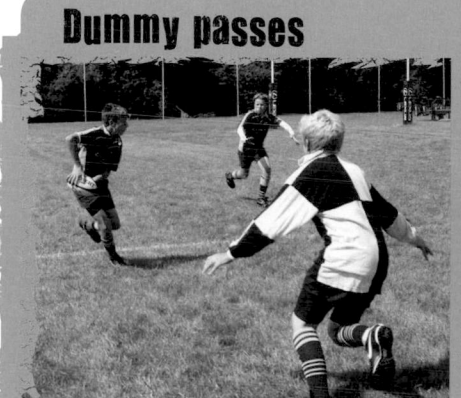  

1 The player with the ball swings his arms across his body, pretending to pass to his team-mate who is running just behind him.

2 His opponent realises this and runs towards the receiver, ready to tackle him. At the last minute, the ball passer brings the ball back to his chest.

3 The player with the ball steps to the defender's left side and carries on with the ball, unopposed, while the defender has committed to his tackle.

Ireland's former captain, Brian O'Driscoll side-steps off his left leg to get past the Italian centre, Andrea Masi, during a Six Nations match.

Tackling

In order to stop attacking runners who have the ball, defenders must tackle them. Failing to make a successful tackle will allow the opposition to break the team's defence and could create a try-scoring opportunity.

Keep it low

Tackles must be made below an opponent's shoulders. A tackle above the shoulders will result in a penalty being awarded to the opposition and, if serious enough, the player could be sent off. The most effective place to tackle an opponent is around the legs because the opponent will not be able to run any further. However, as his hands are free, he can still make a pass to a team-mate. Some players prefer to tackle at chest height. Although this can prevent any passes being made, it is risky. If the tackle is weak, the player can push the tackling player away.

Player power
Just before you make contact in a tackle, make sure that you get a low body position. This will put you in the best position to grab your opponent's legs, wrapping them up and making a secure tackle.

Courtney Lawes tackles for Northampton during a match against London Wasps. His low tackle means the Wasps player will be unable to run any further.

From all angles

In most situations, players will find opponents running straight at them. They should be tackled using the front-on tackle (see below). However, players will find themselves in situations during a match where they will need to tackle an opponent from other angles. For example, if chasing down a player who has broken through his team's defence, players will need to tackle the opposition from behind. A tap tackle is used when an opponent is almost past the defender. This last-ditch tackle involves tapping the ball carrier's foot or ankle in order to make him stumble and drop the ball.

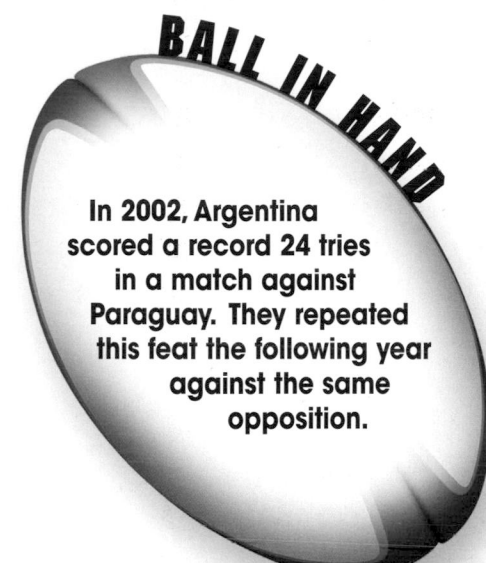

BALL IN HAND

In 2002, Argentina scored a record 24 tries in a match against Paraguay. They repeated this feat the following year against the same opposition.

Front-on tackle

The tackler crouches down in front of the ball carrier. He uses his right shoulder to drive into his opponent and keeps his arms wrapped around his opponent's legs. The opponent will have no option but to fall.

From-behind tackle

The tackler makes contact with the ball carrier from behind. He puts his head to one side of his opponent's leg and wraps his arms around his legs. When the player falls, the tackler will try to land on him to avoid injury.

Side-on tackle

The tackler drives into the ball carrier from the side, putting his bodyweight into the tackle. His head slips behind the hips of the player he is tackling and he keeps his arms around the player's legs to bring him to the ground.

Being tackled

Once players have been tackled, it is important that they move into the correct position so their team can keep possession of the ball. Failing to do this can see an attack grind to a halt or see the opposition steal possession and launch an attack.

Keep it live

Before being tackled, players should be aware of where their team-mates are on the pitch. To help with this, team-mates should shout to let the player with the ball know where they are. Then, if a tackle is made, the tackled player has the opportunity to make a quick, short pass, or 'off-load'. This allows play to continue without a break-down forming. A break-down could give the opposition time to organise its defence.

This Stade Montois player is looking to make a quick off-load to stop a break-down from forming.

Presenting the ball

1 The ball carrier has been tackled to the ground by his opponent and cannot pass back to a team-mate. He must release the ball as soon as he is on the ground.

2 He places the ball away from his body, towards his own team-mates and away from opposition defenders. A team-mate can then collect it and keep possession.

Presenting the ball

When a player is tackled, it may not be possible to throw a quick pass: team-mates may be too far away, or the player may have been tackled around the arms. When this happens, players need to get their body into the right position. If they stay on their feet, they should turn to face their team-mates. This gives them the chance to grab the ball and wrestle it back. If a player is tackled to the floor, he should turn to face his own team and place the ball on the floor back towards his own team-mates.

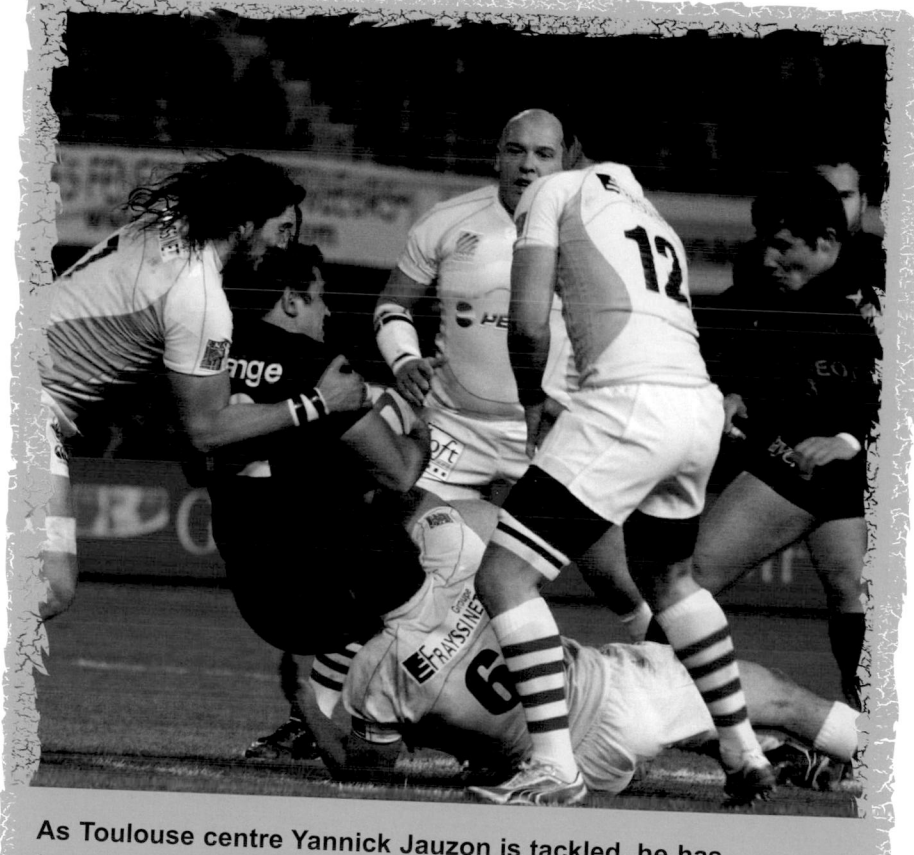

As Toulouse centre Yannick Jauzon is tackled, he has turned to face his team-mates. He is looking to place the ball so that his team-mates can pick it up.

Rucking and mauling

Once someone has been tackled, the two sets of players compete to win possession. This period is known as the break-down and can see some ferocious competition between teams. Defenders will try to steal the ball while attackers look to keep possession.

On the floor

If the tackled player has been thrown to the floor, then a ruck forms. The tackled player must release the ball. Other players are not allowed to handle the ball, unless their team-mates have pushed the opposition away and they are picking up the ball to pass it away or run. If performed well, a ruck can be completed quickly, giving the opposition little time to organise its defence.

Player power

Rugby players must 'play to the referee'. This means not stopping play until you hear the referee's whistle. Referees will regularly let play carry on, even if a law has been broken, usually if the team that did not break the law has the ball. This is called 'playing advantage'.

Perpignan players (in red) crouch low to join a ruck and push the opposition clear of the ball.

On your feet

If the tackled player has stayed on his feet, then a maul forms. Attacking team-mates will secure the ball and then form up, or bind, on either side. This prevents the opposition from reaching around and grabbing the ball. As with a ruck, players joining a maul should keep a low body position and a straight back. This makes it easier to push opposition players. It is also very important that attacking team-mates talk to each other so that everyone knows who has the ball and what they should be doing.

Defending players will first try to turn the tackled player so that he is facing away from his team-mates. This makes it easier to steal the ball. If this is not possible, they will try to slow down the speed with which the attacking players can complete the maul.

> **Because defensive lines are so tight in the modern game, the open-side's role is turning rucks and mauls into continuity play again.**
>
> Former New Zealand number eight
> **Zinzan Brooke**

Maul

1 The ball carrier is tackled but manages to stay on his feet. His team-mates rush to support him.

2 The tackled player turns to face his team-mates so that the opposition cannot get to the ball. The supporting team-mates form a maul.

3 The players in the maul push to drive forwards, gaining possession as they do so. In the meantime, the ball is grappled to the back of the maul, away from the opposition.

Kicking

Any player can kick the ball during a rugby match. However, kicks are usually taken by one of the backs, such as the fly-half.

Kicking for goal

There are three points-scoring kicks: a penalty, a drop kick and a conversion. For each kick to be successful, the ball must travel over the crossbar and between the two uprights. Penalties are awarded to a team when an opposition player has broken one of the laws. If the penalty is within a kicker's range of the posts, then his team can choose to kick at goal. Drop kicks are kicks out of the player's hand and are taken during open play.

Drop kick

1 To make a successful drop kick, the player releases the ball and at the same time, takes back his kicking foot.

2 He keeps his head down and his weight on his standing leg as he times his kick to connect with the ball just after it bounces.

3 While the ball travels in the air, the player's kicking foot swings through to complete a high follow through.

A kicking tee holds the ball in place while Danny Cipriani takes a penalty. He keeps his right leg firmly planted as he kicks with his left.

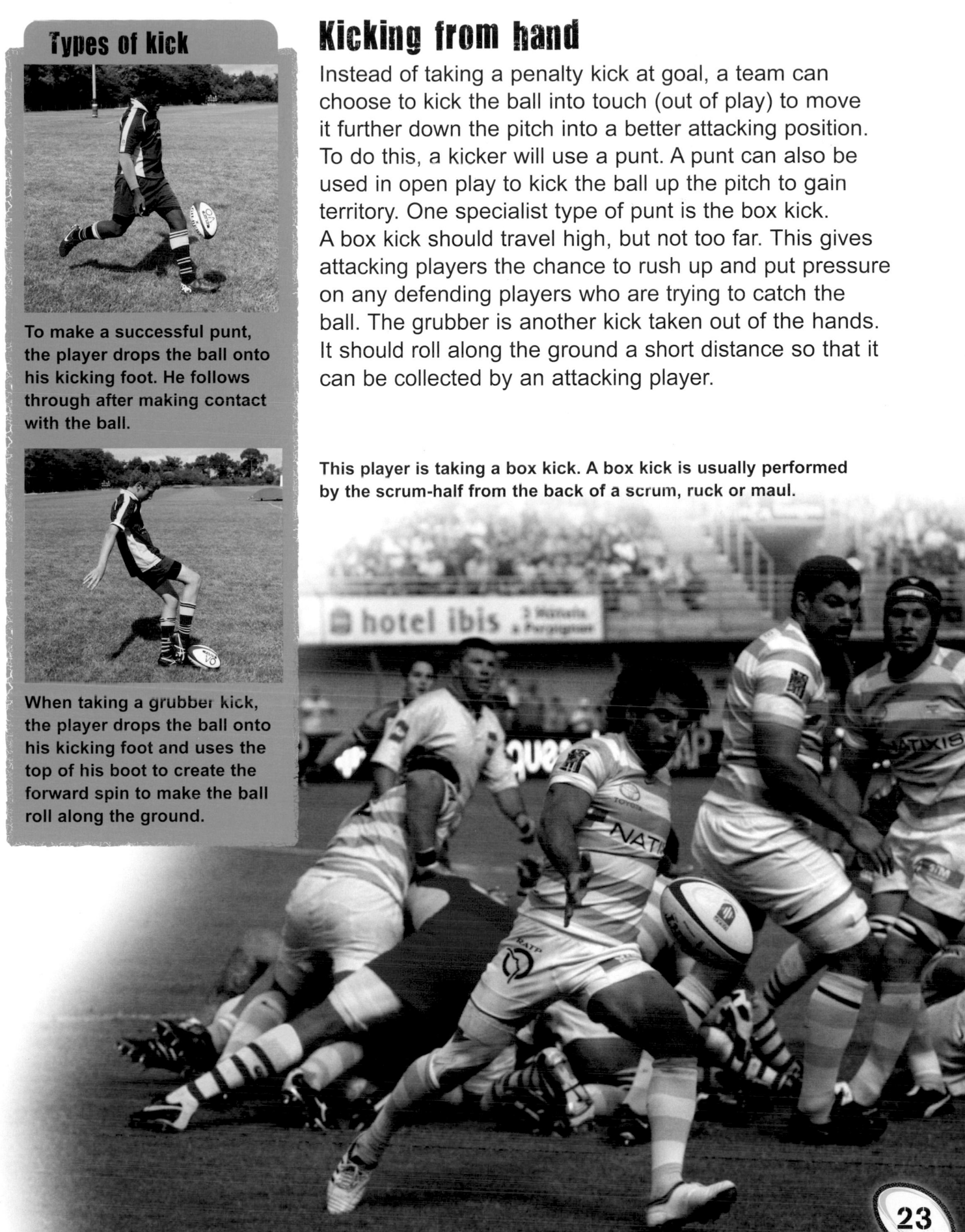

To make a successful punt, the player drops the ball onto his kicking foot. He follows through after making contact with the ball.

When taking a grubber kick, the player drops the ball onto his kicking foot and uses the top of his boot to create the forward spin to make the ball roll along the ground.

Kicking from hand

Instead of taking a penalty kick at goal, a team can choose to kick the ball into touch (out of play) to move it further down the pitch into a better attacking position. To do this, a kicker will use a punt. A punt can also be used in open play to kick the ball up the pitch to gain territory. One specialist type of punt is the box kick. A box kick should travel high, but not too far. This gives attacking players the chance to rush up and put pressure on any defending players who are trying to catch the ball. The grubber is another kick taken out of the hands. It should roll along the ground a short distance so that it can be collected by an attacking player.

This player is taking a box kick. A box kick is usually performed by the scrum-half from the back of a scrum, ruck or maul.

Catching and fielding

At certain times during a rugby match, players will have to catch or field a loose ball. Players need to develop specific skills so that they can secure and control the ball in all of these situations.

The high ball

When catching or fielding a loose ball, players need to keep their eyes on it at all times. When catching a ball from a high kick, it is important for players to give themselves a secure base by planting their feet wide apart. Players should try to turn side-on to the ball, so that if the ball is dropped, it is more likely to bounce sideways or backwards. If it bounces forwards, the referee would stop play for a knock-on and award a scrum to the opposition.

Some players try to leap high to catch a ball. This may prevent the opposition from tackling the catcher, but it is easier for the player to drop the ball if he is off his feet.

To catch a high kick, this player has moved to stand under the ball and has planted his feet firmly on the ground. While keeping his eyes on the ball, he raises his arms and keeps his elbows bent, ready to catch it and bring the ball back into his chest.

The low ball

Unlike a round football, the oval rugby ball will roll and bounce at odd angles. Fielding a rolling rugby ball requires a great deal of concentration. The safest way to field a rolling ball is to slide onto the ground and collect the ball between your arms and body. Trying to pick up the ball while running is a faster way of securing possession as you are on your feet, but it is risky and you could easily spill the ball and lose possession.

Sliding

1 To field the rolling ball by sliding, the player has sprinted to it.

2 He drops to the floor and gets his hands on the ball. By holding his hand over the ball, if he fumbles, the ball will go backwards, avoiding a knock-on.

3 With the ball under control, the player rolls over to face forwards. Once he is on his feet he will be in the right direction to continue the attack.

The lineout

Lineouts are used to restart a match when the ball goes out of play. They involve individual skills, including accurate throwing, jumping and lifting. Players need to coordinate these skills to act as a unit to win the ball cleanly.

Throwing in

The hooker usually throws in the ball at a lineout. He has to make sure that the ball is thrown in at the right speed and height so that the team-mate who is jumping in the lineout, is able to catch the ball cleanly. The ball must also be thrown in straight between the two lines of players. If it is not, the referee will award the opposition the chance to have a scrum or to take the lineout themselves.

Most players throw the ball with two hands to help with accuracy. They hold it overhead so that their team-mates can see when the ball is coming.

jumping and lifting

At older age groups, players are able to lift jumpers in the lineout. They usually hold the jumper around the shorts or his thighs and lift him above the heads of the opposition. For younger age groups, lifting is not allowed, and players have to jump on their own to catch the ball.

Once the ball has been caught, the jumper can tap the ball back to his scrum-half, who usually stands just by the lineout. Alternatively, he can wait for his team-mates to form a maul (see page 21) around him and push the opposition players back.

Forming a maul

1 Seven players from each team line up for the throw in. The hooker throws the ball just high enough for his team-mate to catch it cleanly.

2 The ball-catcher holds the ball securely while his team-mates move to form a maul. The maul enables the team to drive forwards.

Tapping the ball back

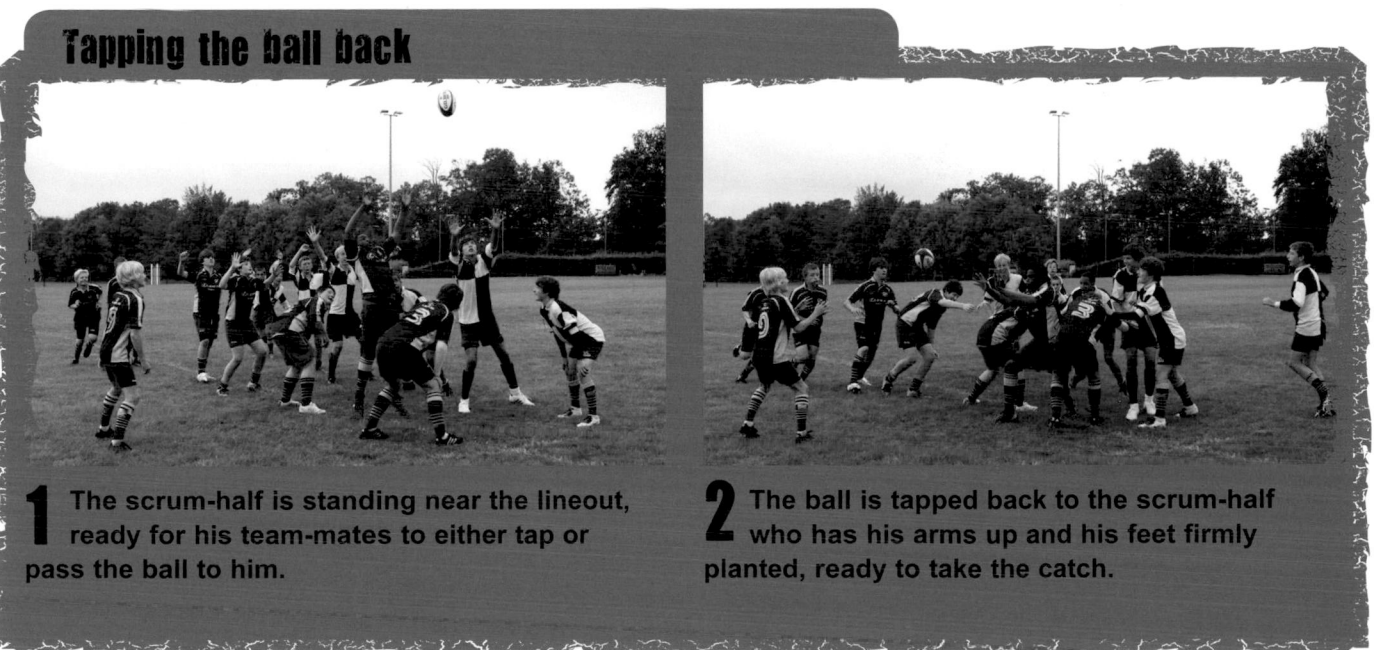

1 The scrum-half is standing near the lineout, ready for his team-mates to either tap or pass the ball to him.

2 The ball is tapped back to the scrum-half who has his arms up and his feet firmly planted, ready to take the catch.

The scrum

Scrums are used to restart play when the ball has been passed or dropped forwards and when a ruck or maul has stalled. The eight forwards join, or bind, together before engaging with the opposition's forwards.

Acting as one

Binding together tightly is probably the most important factor when scrummaging. A team that has not bound tightly together will not be able to push as a unit, and may be shoved back off the ball by the opposition. First to bind are the hooker and the two props. The two second row forwards then join, followed by the flankers and the number eight (see right). Once bound, the players will make sure that they are in a good position to push against the opposition.

These two scrums have bound together tightly and are crouched low, keeping their shoulders above their waists. The two front rows engage with their heads to the left (see above).

Feed and strike

Once they have engaged, neither group of forwards can push until the ball has been fed into the scrum. This is the job of the scrum-half, who must roll the ball down the centre of the scrum. The hooker can then strike the ball back towards the rear of his own scrum. Here the ball is controlled by the number eight using his feet. If the scrum is stable or moving forwards, the attacking side then has the option of the scrum-half passing the ball out to the backs, or the number eight can pick up the ball and charge towards the opposition.

These players are using a scrummaging machine to practise their technique. Each player needs to crouch low with his shoulders above his waist, keeping his back flat and his knees bent.

Never practise scrummaging without a coach present.

Scrum

1 The scrum-half is ready to feed the ball into the middle of the scrum.

2 Once fed in, the hooker uses this foot to roll back the ball to the number eight.

3 The number eight gets the ball to the scrum-half, who passes it out to one of the backs.

What it takes to be...

A top player

Bryan Habana

Renowned for his strong running style, Habana made his international debut at the age of 21. During his career, he has won every competition a South African rugby player can, including the Currie Cup (the South African cup competition), the Super 14, the Tri Nations, he has beaten the British and Irish Lions and won the World Cup in 2007.

Career path

- 2003–2004 Makes his debut for the South African sevens team.

- 2004 Makes his debut for the Golden Lions in the Currie Cup.

- 2004 Makes his debut for the full South African team.

- 2005 Moves to the Blue Bulls Super 12 team. Makes his Tri-Nations debut. Shortlisted for the IRB World Player of the Year. Selected by SA Rugby as South African Player of the Year.

- 2007 Wins the Super 14 final. Wins the World Cup with South Africa. Named IRB International Player of the Year.

During the 2007 Rugby World Cup in France, Habana scored eight tries to equal the record for a single tournament. South Africa went on to win the tournament.

Glossary

backs the group of seven players who line up behind the forwards and are involved in attacking moves.

break-down the period immediately after a tackle has been made.

dummy a technique where a player pretends to perform a move to trick a defender.

forwards the group of eight players who are involved in scrums and lineouts.

knock-on when the ball touches the hand or arm of a player and moves forwards and touches the ground as a result.

maul a formation of players brought around the ball carrier, who is still in possession of the ball and has not been brought to the ground.

off-loading getting rid of the ball, usually by passing.

open play play not from a set-piece.

physiotherapist a medical person who uses massage and exercises to ensure players are fit and able to play.

possession when a team has the ball under control.

ruck a loose formation of players created around a free ball, or a player with the ball who has been tackled to the ground.

set-piece a term used to describe restart moves, such as line-outs and scrums.

side-step a sudden change of sideways direction. Side-steps are used to get past a defender.

Books

Training to Succeed: Rugby by Rita Story (Franklin Watts, 2009)
Sporting Skills: Rugby by Clive Gifford (Wayland, 2008)
Inside Sport: Rugby by Clive Gifford (Wayland, 2007)

Websites

www.aru.rugby.com.au/onlinecoaching
The online coaching pages of the Australian Rugby Union's website are full of lessons, drills and tips to improve skills.

www.planet-rugby.com
An international website with coverage of leagues, cups and national teams from all over the world.

Index